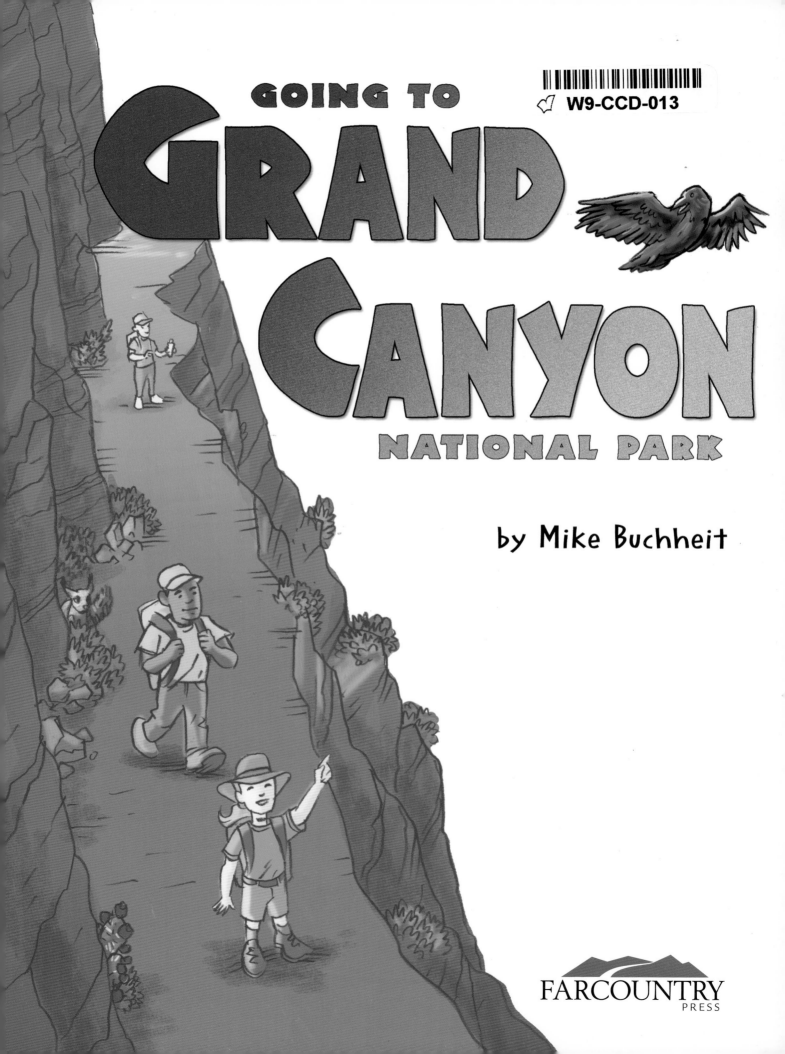

GOING TO GRAND CANYON

NATIONAL PARK

by Mike Buchheit

FARCOUNTRY
PRESS

W9-CCD-013

This book is dedicated to my amazing nieces and nephews with their delightfully contagious curiosity and sense of wonder.

Acknowledgments

Special thanks for inspiration and fact-checking goes out to Kim Buchheit, Tom and Sandy Pittenger, Wayne Ranney, Jack Pennington, and my colleagues and friends in the Division of Science and Resource Management at Grand Canyon National Park.

Many thanks as well to this book's editor Jessica Solberg, designer Shirley Machonis, and illustrator Robert Rath.

ISBN 10: 1-56037-515-9
ISBN 13: 978-1-56037-515-9

© 2012 by Farcountry Press
Text © 2012 by Mike Buchheit

For more information on our books, write Farcountry Press, P.O. Box 5630, Helena, MT 59604; call (800) 821-3874; or visit www.farcountrypress.com.

Library of Congress Cataloging-in-Publication Data

Buchheit, Mike.
  Going to Grand Canyon National Park / by Mike Buchheit.
      p. cm.
  Includes index.
  ISBN-13: 978-1-56037-515-9
  ISBN-10: 1-56037-515-9
1. Grand Canyon National Park (Ariz.)--Juvenile literature. I. Title.
  F788.B79 2012
  979.1'32--dc23
                              2011025980

Created, produced, and designed in the United States.
Manufactured by   Everbest Printing
                      334 Huanshi Road South
                      Dachong Western Industrial District
                      Panyu, Guangdong, China
                      January 2012
                      Printed in China.

16 15 14 13 12   1 2 3 4 5

Table of Contents

Get the BIG Picture

"Cool!" "Awesome!" "Unbelievable!" On any given day along the rim of the world's most famous canyon, you're bound to hear these words—probably in a dozen languages.

Once in awhile you can overhear someone joke, "Oh, it's just a big hole in the ground." At 277 river miles (446 km) long and 10 miles (16 km) wide, they are certainly right about that. But Grand Canyon is much, much more!

Grand Canyon as seen from a satellite orbiting the Earth

Grand Canyon is one of the few land features on Earth that you can see from space. It is also one of the "crown jewels" of the national park system, a homeland for American Indian tribes, critical habitat for plants and animals, a virtual laboratory for researchers, a classroom for educators, a playground for hikers, backpackers, and rafters, and often ranked as one of the Seven Natural Wonders of the world.

As you turn the pages of this book, you'll discover what makes Grand Canyon such a remarkable place—and why we should all protect it for future generations. Together, we'll climb ancient rocks, spot amazing plants, track awesome animals, and go back in time to see how early pioneers and native peoples lived.

Get ready for a wild adventure because we're Going to Grand Canyon National Park!

Grand

North Kaibab Trailhead

Grand Canyon Lodge

Bright Angel Point

Ribbon Falls

Phantom Ranch

Hermit Rapid

Yavapai Geology Museum

Mather Point

Yaki Point

Grand Canyon Village

South Kaibab Trailhead

Mohave Point

Hopi Point

Pima Point

Hermits Rest

GRAND CANYON NATIONAL PARK

GRAND CANYON NATIONAL PARK

area shown

Canyon

Roosevelt Point

Walhalla Overlook

Cape Royal

Vishnu Temple

Cape Solitude

Comanche Point

Lipan Point

Desert View Watchtower

Moran Point

Grandview Point

South Rim

Tusayan Ruin

COLORADO RIVER

DESERT VIEW DRIVE

Geology Rocks!

*D*ude. Grand Canyon National Park rangers use this word a lot. Is it because they're trying to sound cool? Perhaps. But they also use this word to explain how Grand Canyon was created. It's as simple as D-U-D-E.

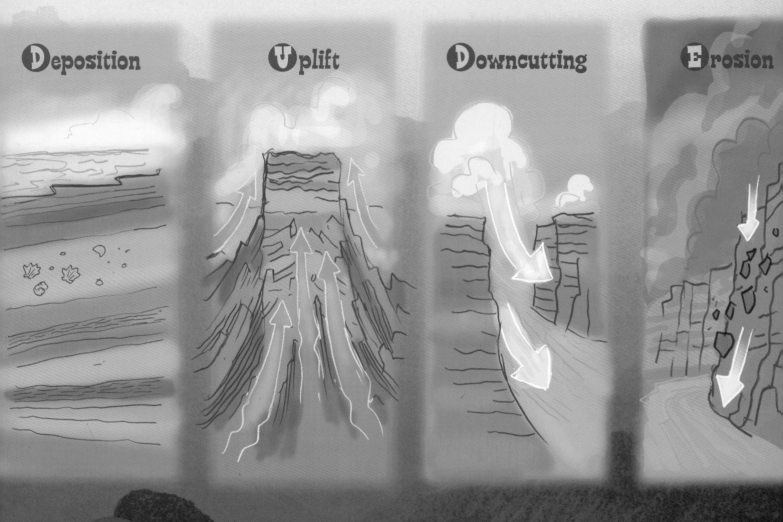

Deposition **Uplift** **Downcutting** **Erosion**

D *is for deposition.* This explains how most of the rock you see arrived here. Over billions of years, wind, water, and gravity deposited sand, mud, rocks, and seashells, forming the many layers you now see in the canyon. Other rocks formed from magma pushed up from Earth's red-hot mantle.

U *is for uplift.* Around 40 to 70 million years ago, the entire Grand Canyon region was uplifted as the crust of the planet buckled.

8

Geology is the study of the Earth, the stuff that makes up the Earth and its structure, and the processes that act upon it.

Geologists work to understand the history of our planet. The better they can understand Earth's history, the better they can foresee how events of the past might influence the future.

Ancient volcanoes pushed lava into the western part of Grand Canyon, creating **giant dams** that backed up the river. The biggest dam was about 2,000 feet (610 m) high and created a lake that was almost 400 miles (644 km) long. This happened more than a dozen times in the past 630,000 years. As more water flowed into these newly formed lakes, they eventually rose high enough to spill over the dams, and then wore them back down through erosion. Other dams simply broke apart, sending towering floods downstream.

There are three basic types of rock: **sedimentary**, **igneous**, and **metamorphic**. Grand Canyon has all three.

Sedimentary rock

Sedimentary rock is created when material such as sand, mud, gravel, or seashells piles up and is squeezed together. Most of the rocks you see in the upper portions of Grand Canyon are sedimentary.

Igneous rock

Igneous rock is formed through the cooling and hardening of magma (or lava, as magma is called if it emerges from the ground) that is pushed up from deep beneath the Earth's surface. Igneous is a Latin word that means "fire."

Metamorphic rock

Metamorphic rock forms deep underground when heat and pressure "cook" either sedimentary or igneous rock. The oldest rock in the canyon is Elves Chasm gneiss, a metamorphic rock that is more than 1.8 billion years old.

D **is for downcutting.** When land is pushed higher, nature wears it back down. The tools for downcutting are wind and water. Between 6 and 8 million years ago, the Colorado River began to slowly slice into the uplifted layers of rock like a knife cuts through butter.

E **is for erosion.** As this newly carved canyon got deeper, erosion caused the sides to cave in and tumble to the river. The river carried the eroded material downstream, often as far as the Gulf of California, which feeds into the Pacific Ocean. Erosion can be caused by rain, freezing and thawing, expanding tree roots, and even earthquakes.

Miners came to Grand Canyon for the **copper, asbestos,** and **silver** found underground. Believe it or not, they also came for the **bat poop!** Bat droppings, or guano, make excellent fertilizer for plants.

Did you know there are **fossils** in Grand Canyon? The **seashells, tube worm burrows,** and **reptile tracks** found here are much older than dinosaurs.

The oldest visible fossils are **stromatolites.** These fossils were once mushroom-shaped colonies of algae that lived near the shore in ancient seas. Stromatolites and other algae used the power of sunlight to combine carbon dioxide and water to make food, releasing oxygen and creating an atmosphere friendly to animals and humans. (Take a deep breath and thank them.) Some stromatolite fossils may be more than 3 billion years old, although the ones in Grand Canyon are closer to 1 billion years old. Live stromatolite colonies grow today in places like Shark Bay, Australia, and the Bahamas.

Copper

Silver

Asbestos

Bat guano

Fossilized worm trails in Bright Angel Shale

Fern imprint on Hermit Shale

These fossilized tracks in Coconino Sandstone are believed to be from an ancient reptile running across a sand dune perhaps 275 million years ago—before dinosaurs walked the earth!

Trilobite in Bright Angel Shale

Geologists have a clever way of teaching the basic rock layers of the canyon. They use the phrase **"Know The Canyon's History, Study Rocks Made By Time."** The first letter in each word corresponds to the first letter in a canyon rock layer.

What did the limestone boulder say to the geologist? "Don't take me for granite!"

KNOW	**KAIBAB** LIMESTONE
THE	**TOROWEAP** FORMATION
CANYON'S	**COCONINO** SANDSTONE
HISTORY	**HERMIT** SHALE
STUDY	**SUPAI** FORMATION
ROCKS	**REDWALL** LIMESTONE
MADE	**MUAV** LIMESTONE
BY	**BRIGHT ANGEL** SHALE
TIME	**TAPEATS** SANDSTONE

270 million years ago
273 million years ago
275 million years ago
280 million years ago
285-315 million years ago
340 million years ago
505 million years ago
515 million years ago
525 million years ago

Colorado River

CHECK IT OUT!

Every step you take down into the canyon takes you back **thousands of years** in geologic time.

The Wonders of Water

Water is life. Nowhere is this more obvious than between the towering walls of Grand Canyon. Every drop of water is as precious as gold to the desert plants and animals found here.

The rim of the canyon receives between fifteen and twenty-five inches (38–64 cm) of precipitation each year (the lower and warmer canyon receives much less). Half of the rim's precipitation comes in the form of summer rain, and half as winter snow. Between the snow and rain are weeks or months of drought. When rain and snow falls, it trickles into cracks in the ground and filters down through hundreds of feet of rock layers. When the water reaches a rock layer that it can't flow through, like shale, it moves sideways and finds its way back to the surface. These special places where the water bubbles to the surface are called springs and seeps. Many of the canyon's plants and animals rely on this water for life.

The Colorado River is the main source of water in Grand Canyon. It flows 1,450 miles (2,334 km) from its origin in the Rocky Mountains of Colorado all the way to the Gulf of California in northern Mexico. Along its path it drops 14,000 feet (4,267 m) in elevation—that's almost a three-mile (4.8 km) drop! As the river tumbles to the ocean, it sculpts several beautiful canyons, including Grand Canyon.

Ribbon Falls

Vasey's Paradise

Colorado River

The Colorado River has *two big jobs*. The first is to *carve*. The second is to *carry*.

For the past 6 to 8 million years, the river has been carving deeper and deeper. It sliced more quickly at first, as it cut through the softer rock of the upper layers. The process is much slower today as it wears away the super-hard rock of the lower layers. Every year, the canyon gets deeper by about the thickness of a sheet of paper.

The river also carries stuff downstream. This includes sand, gravel, dirt, and plant material washed into the river by wind and water, thus making the canyon deeper.

The Colorado River also carries more than 25,000 people in rafts through Grand Canyon every year. With big sandy beaches, and more than 100 whitewater rapids, rafting the Colorado River is considered the adventure of a lifetime.

Rafting the Colorado River

SAVING THE HUMPBACK CHUB

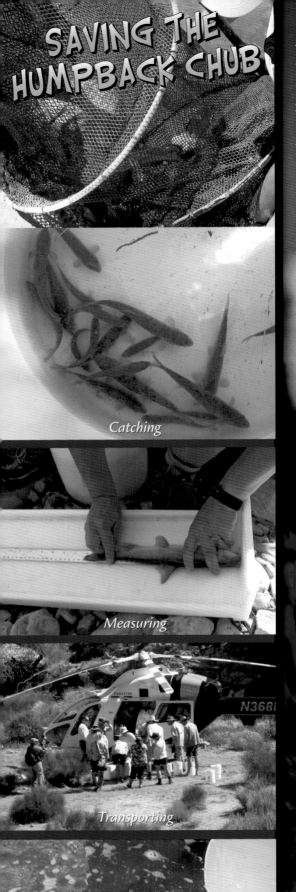

Catching

Measuring

Transporting

N368

Releasing

A dam is a wall built to hold back the water of a river. Glen Canyon Dam was built on the Colorado River and sits fifteen miles (24 km) above Grand Canyon. The Glen Canyon Dam is more than seventy stories tall—that's about twenty school buses stacked end to end.

The water in the depths of Grand Canyon used to be warm and muddy. Now, the water that comes through the dam and into Grand Canyon is from the bottom of Lake Powell, and it is very cold. The fish that live in warm and muddy water find it difficult to live in Grand Canyon. One of these fish, the endangered humpback chub, is still fighting to survive. They now live mostly in warmer side streams. Biologists are working hard to save them, relocating them to places such as Havasu Creek.

Have you noticed that **Havasu Creek** and the **Little Colorado River** are the color of a robin's egg? The beautiful turquoise color comes from a mineral called **calcium carbonate,** which leaches out from the limestone rock beside these desert streams.

Havasu Creek

Crack! Boom! Summer storms in Grand Canyon are loud and flashy. Afternoon cloudbursts, thunder, and lightning happen somewhere in the canyon almost every day during the summer. These downpours can cause flash floods in low-lying places, so be sure to stay high and dry during the monsoon season (early July through early September).

CHECK IT OUT!

The water that comes out of the **faucets** in Grand Canyon National Park originates in **Roaring Springs,** thousands of feet below the North Rim. Since the 1960s, its waters have been pumped out of the canyon through miles of high-pressure pipeline.

Why is the river rich? Because it has two banks.

15

Fin, Feather, and Fur

It's a crisp September morning as we make our way to the edge of the canyon. With winter approaching, it seems that every creature has a purpose: to mate, migrate, or munch as much food as possible before the snow starts to fall.

Ahhreeeeeeyah! An eerie call is heard in the nearby forest. It's the bugling of an **elk,** the park's largest plant eater. Through the trees, we can see a large-antlered male. His piercing whistle is meant to warn other males. We definitely want to keep our distance, so off we go.

rock squirrel

After a mile or two we drop our packs and take a break on a big sandstone rock. We notice some strange shapes in the mud at our feet: they are the tracks of a **mountain lion.** It was probably hunting for **gray fox, jackrabbits,** or **deer.** Only about twenty-five mountain lions live in or near Grand Canyon. They rarely bother humans, but their tracks remind us to stay alert as we head down the trail.

mountain lion tracks

gray fox

As we pick up our packs, we startle a **rock squirrel** trying to get at our food. These fearless rodents will do just about anything for a handout. But we know better. We remember the ranger telling us to keep our food away from *all* wildlife in order to keep them wild and healthy. Rock squirrels are bolder than the Abert and Kaibab squirrels that live in the dense forests above. These two tree squirrels have tufts of hair, or tassels, on the tips of their ears.

It is believed that at one time the Abert and Kaibab squirrels were the same species. But as the canyon grew warmer, the forest that once connected the North and South Rims turned to impassable desert. Now isolated on either rim, the Abert (South Rim) and Kaibab (North Rim) squirrels evolved differently due to the slight variations in their shrinking habitat. Today they are more like cousins that never get to visit each other.

elk

mule deer

Abert squirrel

As we step onto the trail, we spot a **mule deer** scampering into the brush. Unlike the elk that only live in the forest, these long-eared beauties can be found from rim to river.

Just below the rim we see flocks of **pinyon jays.** They are getting ready to fly to warmer climates after a busy summer collecting and burying pinyon nuts, their sole source of food. They hide these snacks so they can munch on them when they return the following spring. Sometimes the birds forget where they buried the nuts, which then sprout into new pinyon trees. By their forgetfulness, they help produce trees that will feed other jays for years to come.

pinyon jays

The closer we get to the bottom of the canyon, the hotter it gets. We spot a **collared lizard** doing push-ups on a rock. We know he is a male because of his bright colors. The reptile lifts himself up and down to create a breeze that will help him cool down, though it looks like he's just showing off his muscles.

collared lizard

As we round a corner, we notice **coyote** scat, or droppings, in a tidy pile atop a flat rock. These tricky scavengers can be found from top to bottom at Grand Canyon. They hunt mostly after dark, and their yelps and howls are one of the more unforgettable sounds in the Arizona night.

A few more twists and turns and we make it to the Colorado River, the rock bottom of the canyon. We watch a **mallard duck** swimming in a calm stretch of water. He's probably eating aquatic plants, or perhaps fishing for small **rainbow trout.** Suddenly he changes from the hunter to the hunted. A **peregrine falcon,** one of the fastest animals on the planet, rockets down from above and narrowly misses in his attempt to catch the startled mallard. That was a close one.

rainbow trout

peregrine falcon

mallard duck

canyon
wrens

The sweet trailing song of the tiny **canyon wren** arrives on a cool breeze just below Indian Garden. These birds inhabit the cliffs in the belly of the canyon. Many hikers believe that your hike in the canyon isn't complete until you hear one.

pink
rattlesnake

mouse

bats

We follow the trail upstream along the Colorado River until we are able to cross its emerald-green waters on a steel footbridge. Soon we're in our campsite at Bright Angel Campground waiting for a stubborn rattlesnake to slither away into the weeds. It is a **Grand Canyon pink rattlesnake,** found only in Grand Canyon, and it's a pretty mellow fellow compared to other types of rattlesnakes. The other good news is that it will be hunting **mice** all night. That will help keep the rodents from trying to get into our tents.

Just for fun we take out our special flashlights to scout for **scorpions.** For reasons that scientists can't quite understand, these stinging arachnids are fluorescent; they glow in the dark under black light. A few can be spotted on the nearby brush, probably hunting insects. Yikes! Better check our boots in the morning to make sure none climbed inside.

scorpion

We fall asleep under an amazing canopy of stars, listening to the chirping **bats** as they go about their business of catching flying insects in the cool evening air.

HAVE YOU SEEN THESE ANIMALS?

☐ elk

☐ mule deer

☐ pinyon jay

☐ gray fox

☐ jackrabbit

☐ rock squirrel

☐ Abert squirrel

☐ Kaibab squirrel

☐ collared lizard

☐ bighorn sheep

☐ coyote

☐ pink rattlesnake

Park wildlife biologists are aware of more than two dozen **mountain lions** that live in the forest along the South Rim. These predators are seldom seen. Many wear radio collars so researchers can monitor their movements. One was tracked traveling all the way across the canyon—a feat that included a dangerous swim across the Colorado River!

Mountain lion

Biologists released **California condors** in the Vermilion Cliffs north of Grand Canyon in 1996 in an attempt to re-establish this endangered scavenger in the region. One of the largest birds in the world, adult condors have a wingspan of nine feet (2.7 m). They visit Grand Canyon in the summer, gliding on the warm air that rises out of the canyon in the afternoon. Once almost extinct, now nearly 200 condors are flying free in the skies of the western United States and northern Mexico. An equal number are still in captivity awaiting their release.

Condor

TRY THIS:

What's your **wingspan**? Have a friend measure your outstretched arms from fingertip to fingertip. For most people this is the exact same measurement as their height.

CHECK IT OUT!

Everyone knows a group of elk is called a herd. But did you know that a group of ants is called an army? What do you call a group of owls? Check out this list of strange names for groups of animals:

a **parliament** of owls
a **parcel** of deer
a **generation** of vipers
a **scurry** of squirrels
a **lounge** of lizards
a **scold** of jays
a **hover** of trout
a **band** of coyotes

Rainbow trout can weigh up to ten pounds, and they eat mostly insects. They spawn in big side streams throughout the canyon, where they have become an important food source for bald eagles that spend the winter in Grand Canyon.

Rainbow trout

Bark scorpion

Ranger's rule of thumb: If the thumb of your outstretched arm cannot completely block the view of a nearby animal, you are too close.

The most common scorpion in Grand Canyon is the **bark scorpion.** These creepy critters are only about an inch long and pale in color, making them difficult to see. Scorpions eat insects and will only sting to protect them-selves. The venom of the bark scorpion is rather strong, so they can be quite dangerous. They are most active at night and like to crawl into tight spaces, so be sure to shake out anything left outside your tent overnight. The best way to keep from being stung is to avoid walking around barefoot.

Scientists have recorded many kinds of animals living in Grand Canyon National Park.

NUMBER OF SPECIES
256 BIRDS
91 MAMMALS
17 FISH
57 REPTILES AND AMPHIBIANS
33 CRUSTACEANS
37 MOLLUSKS

What did the naughty little diamondback rattlesnake say to his big sister? "Don't be such a rattle-tail."

A *tarantula hawk* is a large wasp that hunts tarantulas as food for its offspring. Using its large stinger, a female tarantula hawk paralyzes the spider and lays an egg inside its body. When the wasp baby hatches, it digs around inside the spider and feeds on it for several weeks until the wasp reaches adulthood.

A tarantula hawk sting can be very painful, but the good news is that they tend not to sting humans unless they are being bothered.

Roots and Shoots

We met many interesting creatures on our hike into the canyon. On our way up to the North Rim, let's turn our attention to the amazing plants and trees along the North Kaibab Trail. We'll see a wide variety of vegetation based on elevation, temperature, and the availability of water.

We begin our hike beneath the rustling leaves of a **cottonwood tree.** These thirsty giants can be found beside side streams throughout the canyon. The cottonwoods at Bright Angel Campground were planted many years ago to provide shade for tired hikers. Joining them in dense thickets along Bright Angel Creek are **willow, hackberry,** and **cattail.**

cottonwood

willow

cattail

hackberry

utah agave

For thousands of years American Indians have found ways to use canyon plants for food, medicine, and building materials. After a mile or two we encounter a favorite, the **Utah agave.** Native people would harvest the core, or heart, of these sharp-leaved plants and roast them underground using heated rocks. After several days of cooking, these agave hearts would be tender enough to eat. Their taste has been compared to sweet potatoes.

prickly pear cactus

columbine

prickly pear cactus

Just a stone's throw from the creek, things change quickly. Here beneath the hot sun, the scratchy desert plants take over. As we stroll by historic Phantom Ranch, we reach a patch of **prickly pear cactus**, one of two dozen species of cacti in the canyon. Nearly every pad has produced a fruit that resembles a small plum. These make tasty jam if you know the recipe, but watch out for the tiny sharp spines!

moss

maidenhair fern

monkeyflower

juniper

After a quick visit to Ribbon Falls, a tumbling waterfall surrounded by **moss, monkeyflower, maidenhair fern,** and **columbine**, the trail gets steeper. Plants called **Mormon tea** line our path. This spiny shrub contains ephedrine, a chemical that has been used to treat asthma and the common cold.

A few miles from the top, we begin to encounter sturdy **juniper trees**. Though only twenty feet (6 m) high, these trees can be hundreds of years old.

Mormon tea

pinyon pine

quaking aspen

Western bluebird

Higher still are the **pinyon pine trees.** Loaded with fat, calories, and protein, pinyon nuts were an important food for the American Indians. Squirrels, mice, and pinyon jays love them, too.

We know we're near the top when we see the rustling leaves of the **quaking aspen.** Their golden color also tells us that winter is approaching soon. Our heavy breathing reminds us that this is a high-altitude tree, typically found in the mountains where the air is thin.

ponderosa
pine

We are now more than 8,000 feet (2,438 m) above sea level. That's a mile higher in elevation than where we started at Phantom Ranch. The rim of the canyon gets much more rain and snow than the bottom, so its forest is comparatively thick. We brush past towering **ponderosa pines** and **Douglas-firs.**

Douglas-fir

Kaibab
squirrel

Finally we're at the top! Amazingly, at Grand Canyon, a hike from the bottom to the top lets you enjoy the same variety of plants that you might see on a hike along the Pacific Ocean from Mexico to Canada. That's thousands of miles compared to the fourteen we just hiked. But we're so tired it feels like we've hiked a thousand miles.

Utah agave

Cottonwood and prickly pear cactus

Mormon tea

Moss

Pack rat midden

Scientists use the word **biodiversity** to describe the mixture of plants and animals that exist in a given place. Grand Canyon has over 1,700 species of plants, more than any other national park, so it is considered to have great biodiversity.

Sometimes plants from other places are brought here by wind or water, or are carried by humans. These are called **exotic** or **invasive species.** Often they are harmful to the native plants that truly belong here. The National Park Service tries to remove exotic species like the pesky tamarisk tree.

Researchers study the nests, or **middens,** of pack rats in the canyon. In some cases these nests have been continuously used for thousands of years. Pack rats gather objects and pile them up inside their middens. Scientists look at the seeds, twigs, and pollen gathered by these industrious creatures to learn how plants in Grand Canyon have changed over the years.

People of the Canyon

American Indians of the Past and Present

Close your eyes and imagine what it must have been like to be the first person to see Grand Canyon. What a BIG surprise it must have been for the ancient people who had no idea that it was here.

Archaeologists have found **4,300 artifacts** after surveying only **five percent of the park.** They believe that the **first humans arrived** in the canyon region about **12,000 years ago,** not long after the end of the last Ice Age. These people—whom scientists call **Paleo-Indians—** were wandering **hunters** that used big spears to hunt their game, perhaps even the elephant-like **mammoth** that roamed the land at the time. As the large animals became more and more rare, future generations turned to the bow and arrow and snares to catch smaller game. Eventually the growing of **corn, beans,** and **squash** made life a whole lot easier.

For thousands of years, different bands and cultures have come and gone. Some, like a group known as the **Archaic people,** left behind elaborate paintings (**pictographs**) and etchings (**petroglyphs**) of animals and humans on the canyon rocks and walls. Because they didn't build fancy homes, they did not leave much behind for archaeologists to study besides their **stone tools, rock art,** and the occasional **animal figure** created from twigs.

Stone pendant

Tusayan bowl

Archaeologists at work

Shell bead

Pueblo bowl

Split-twig figurine

Many native peoples who have lived in the canyon—from ancient times to today's tribes—have left behind **pictographs** and **petroglyphs**. Do you know the difference?

Pictograph: An ancient or prehistoric drawing or painting on a rock.

Petroglyph: An ancient or prehistoric carving or inscription on a rock.

Pictograph

Petroglyph

Around 1,200 years ago, the **Ancestral Puebloans** arrived in Grand Canyon. They grew **corn, beans,** and **squash, hunted small animals,** made beautiful **baskets** and **pottery,** and lived in tiny **homes made of stone** held together with dried mud. The Ancestral Puebloans left the canyon in the 1200s, perhaps because of a drought. Their descendants, including the **Hopi and Zuni tribes,** still live east of Grand Canyon in their new homelands.

1540
Led by Hopi guides, Spanish explorer Don García López de Cárdenas arrives at the rim of Grand Canyon

1100 C.E.
Hopi establish the village of Oraibi, east of Grand Canyon, thought to be the oldest continuously inhabited settlement in today's United States

2500–500 B.C.E.
Archaic people inhabit the canyon and leave behind split-twig figurines

Circa 12,000 B.C.E.
The first humans arrive at Grand Canyon

800–1250 C.E.
Ancestral Puebloans establish communities in and around Grand Canyon

1185–1225 C.E.
Ancestral Puebloans build and occupy the Tusayan Pueblo on the South Rim

1857–1858
Lieutenant Joseph Christmas Ives leads a military expedition up the Colorado River

TIMELINE OF

After a few more centuries, other tribes moved to the Grand Canyon region, including the Navajo, Paiute, Hualapai, and Havasupai. Each tribe has its own traditions, customs, and folklore. The Hopi tell the story of Tiyo. According to the legend, this young fellow floated through the canyon in a hollow log. At the end of his journey, he met a maiden who taught him the ceremonies needed to bring rain. He married her and the two flew home in a wicker basket to share this valuable teaching with his people.

Billy Burro, a Havasupai Indian

ARCHAEOLOGIST:

A scientist who tries to figure out what life was like long ago by looking at objects (called artifacts) left behind by ancient people.

Mid-1800s
Hunters, trappers, and Mormon settlers are drawn to the North Rim

1883
John Hance becomes the first non-native resident of the Grand Canyon area

1901
First train arrives at Grand Canyon

1869
John Wesley Powell leads the first scientific river exploration into Grand Canyon

1891
Louis Boucher, known as "the Hermit," discovers copper near the Colorado River

1901–1902
Kolb brothers arrive at the South Rim and open their photographic studio specializing in photos of their daring canyon exploits

HUMAN EVENTS

Park rangers ask that visitors not touch any archaeological objects they find. This allows future park visitors to have the same sense of discovery that you had in the park.

The National Park Service recognizes *eleven American Indian tribes* that have current or ancestral ties to Grand Canyon.

The *Havasupai* is the *only tribe whose main village is inside Grand Canyon*. They live beside the turquoise waters of Havasu Creek, which tumbles over a number of major waterfalls on its way to the Colorado River. The only way to get to their village of Supai is by foot, horseback, or helicopter. It's one of the few places left in the country where the mail is still delivered by horse!

Havasu Falls

1905
El Tovar Hotel opens

1908
President Theodore Roosevelt declares Grand Canyon a national monument

1912
Arizona becomes a state

1919
Grand Canyon becomes 17th national park by act of Congress, signed by President Woodrow Wilson

1902
The first automobile arrives in Grand Canyon

1907
Edith Kolb is first pioneer child born at Grand Canyon

1911–1912
Emery and Ellsworth Kolb make a movie about floating the Colorado River

1916
National Park Service created

TIMELINE OF

The first **archaeological dig** at the bottom of Grand Canyon in forty years took place from 2007 to 2009. Archaeologists dug in areas that they knew were used by the canyon's ancient inhabitants. By studying the **pottery, architecture, and baskets** that they found, the scientists learned much about their lifestyle—including the first known use of **cotton** in Grand Canyon.

CHECK IT OUT!

Many of the dwellings built by the canyon's earliest inhabitants **faced south.** Can you figure out why?

In the winter, when the sun is low and to the south, direct sunlight would warm the home with solar energy.

The **Hualapai tribe** built a **platform with a see-through bottom** that hangs over the canyon's edge. The Skywalk is on Hualapai tribal land; it is a four-hour drive from Grand Canyon National Park's South Rim visitor center.

1975
The Grand Canyon Enlargement Act is signed by Gerald Ford, doubling the size of the park

1922
Phantom Ranch is upgraded and renamed by Mary Jane Colter

1956
Congress authorizes construction of the Glen Canyon Dam

1920
The number of people coming to the park by automobile overtakes the number coming by train

1933
Desert View Watchtower, designed by Mary Jane Colter, is completed

1974
Summer bus service begins in order to alleviate traffic jams on the South Rim

1979
Grand Canyon named a World Heritage Site

HUMAN EVENTS

Explorers and Settlers

Explorers

In 1540, a group of **Spanish explorers** led by Don García López de Cárdenas reached Grand Canyon. They were led by **Hopi guides** whose ancestors had known about the canyon for hundreds of years. The Spaniards, the first Europeans to visit Grand Canyon, were investigating reports of a large river in the area. Before returning home, three of the men tried to hike to the bottom of the canyon. They reported that rocks that appeared from a distance to be only as tall as a person were in fact as large as the great tower of Seville back in Spain, more than 300 feet tall (or about 53 people).

More People Arrive

Over the next few centuries, many more explorers came to Grand Canyon in search of fame and fortune. This included two **priests who were trying to find a route** from today's New Mexico to California in 1776, **hunters and pelt-seeking trappers** working the lush forests of the North Rim in the mid-1800s, and **miners** in the late 1800s who used burros to haul copper ore out of the canyon.

John Wesley Powell

The greatest feat in Grand Canyon exploration came when **John Wesley Powell,** a self-taught **geologist** who had lost an arm in the Civil War, **floated the length of the canyon** with his crew of seven men in 1869. Three others began the trip but chose to hike out of the canyon early; they were never seen again. Powell's group was the **first to take boats through this uncharted land** that Powell called **the Great Unknown.** Not long after this mystery was solved, explorers were replaced by **pioneers and settlers.**

John Wesley Powell

Settling Grand Canyon

The first people you might call **tourists** started to arrive in the late 1800s. Many rode mules into Grand Canyon, a tradition that continues to this day.

Wherever there are tourists, businessmen are sure to follow. Soon **tour guides, wranglers, cooks, construction workers, and even photographers** began to trickle to the South Rim in search of adventure, fun, and an honest living. Then along came a train. On September 17, 1901, the **first steam engine train** arrived at the South Rim at what came to be known as Grand Canyon Village, and the modern era began.

Settlers

GREETINGS from GRAND CANYON ARIZ.

CHECK IT OUT!

A mule has a horse for its mother, and a burro (also known as a donkey) for its father.

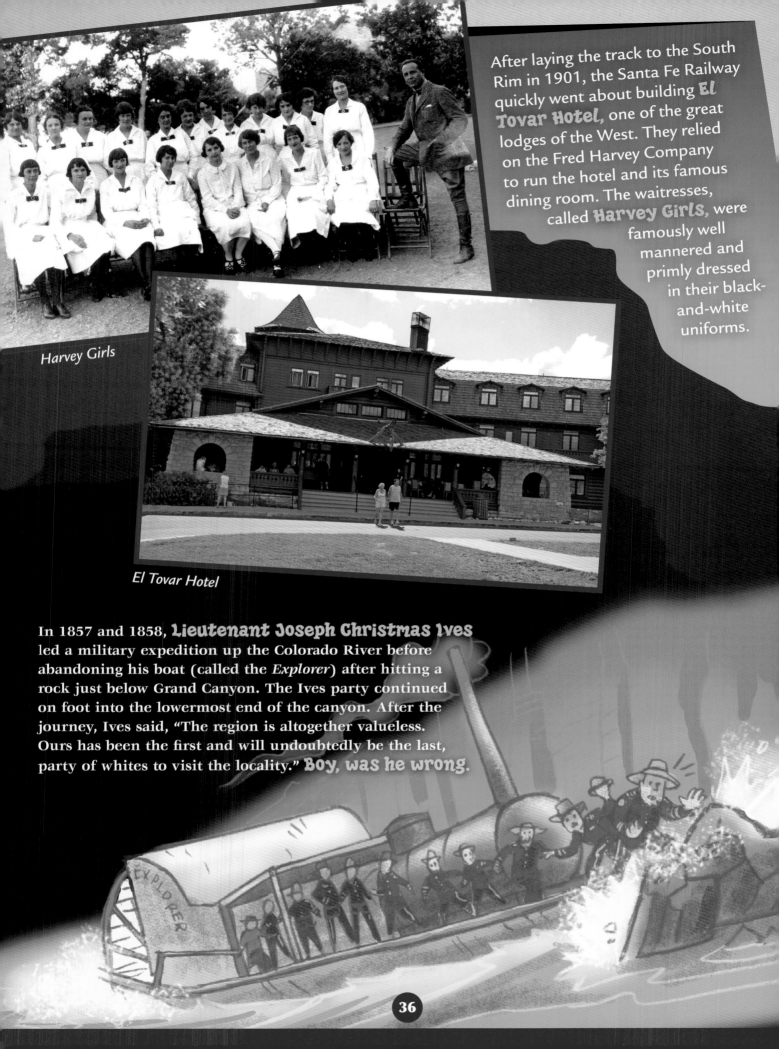

Harvey Girls

After laying the track to the South Rim in 1901, the Santa Fe Railway quickly went about building **El Tovar Hotel,** one of the great lodges of the West. They relied on the Fred Harvey Company to run the hotel and its famous dining room. The waitresses, called **Harvey Girls,** were famously well mannered and primly dressed in their black-and-white uniforms.

El Tovar Hotel

In 1857 and 1858, **Lieutenant Joseph Christmas Ives** led a military expedition up the Colorado River before abandoning his boat (called the *Explorer*) after hitting a rock just below Grand Canyon. The Ives party continued on foot into the lowermost end of the canyon. After the journey, Ives said, "The region is altogether valueless. Ours has been the first and will undoubtedly be the last, party of whites to visit the locality." **Boy, was he wrong.**

The **Kolb brothers** from Pennsylvania were among the earliest pioneers to set up a lasting business on the booming South Rim. *Ellsworth and Emery were photographers, filmmakers, and explorers.* The house they began building in 1904 still stands at the head of the Bright Angel Trail. *The first pioneer child born at Grand Canyon,* Emery's daughter Edith, was carried in and out of the canyon by burro before she was old enough to walk, and *she became the first woman to run a major whitewater rapid in Grand Canyon.*

Mather Point

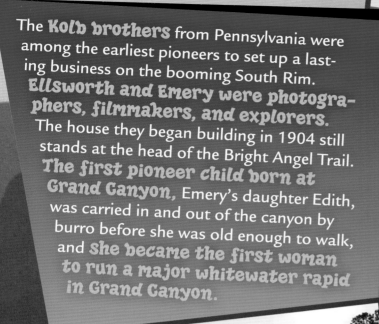

Kolb brothers' studio

The Kolb brothers staged daring photos to draw visitors

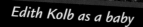

Edith Kolb as a baby

Protecting Grand Canyon

Many men and women have worked hard to protect and preserve Grand Canyon for future generations. These visionaries included President Theodore Roosevelt, who declared Grand Canyon a national monument in 1908. By doing so, he protected the canyon from mining, foresting, and other activities that might damage its fragile resources. "Leave it as it is," he said during a visit in 1903. "You cannot improve on it. The ages have been at work on it, and man can only mar it." He went on to call Grand Canyon the one great thing that every American should see.

#L31
Col. Roosevelts Party Descending Brigh

Roosevelt, at front, descends Bright Angel Trail on horseback

Although Grand Canyon is considered a national treasure, it truly belongs to the people of the world. The United Nations declared it a World Heritage Site in 1979. Today more than thirty percent of the park's visitors are from overseas.

PATRIMONIO MUNDIAL

WORLD HERITAGE • PATRIMOINE MONDIAL

The **National Park Service** (NPS) is the government agency that serves as the caretaker and protector of all the national parks, including Grand Canyon.

More than 400 NPS employees make Grand Canyon National Park a memorable place to visit. Some are rangers that give fun and informative talks to the visiting public. Others are administrators, firefighters, scientists, architects, pilots, bookkeepers, plumbers, heavy machine operators, and law enforcement officers.

The NPS is always looking for people with the right skills who are passionate about nature. If you enjoy your Grand Canyon visit, you might think about making a career in the National Park Service. Who knows, you could become one of more than 2,000 residents that live and work in Grand Canyon National Park year-round.

President Woodrow Wilson

It's Official!

Grand Canyon became the **seventeenth national park** in 1919 thanks to an act of Congress signed by **Woodrow Wilson**. Today, the **1.2 million-acre park ranks eleventh in size**. The park attracts nearly 5 million visitors annually, making it one of the most heavily visited national parks in the country.

FUN FACT

During the pioneer days, a band of thieves used to steal horses in Utah and run them across Grand Canyon. They would sell the horses to un-suspecting buyers in Arizona, then steal more horses, run them back across the canyon, and do the same thing on the other side in Utah.

Your Adventure

As you've discovered, Grand Canyon is a BIG place with lots to see and do. What will you do on your adventure?

Did you know that the park has a **free shuttle bus system** that runs from before dawn to after dusk? Try giving your family car the day off and taking the bus. The handy park newspaper called *The Guide* shows you where all the bus stops are.

The Early Bird...

You know the old saying: The early bird catches the worm! Well, in Grand Canyon, the early bird catches a lot more than worms. **Sunrise—and sunset—at Grand Canyon** are world famous for their beauty. Dawn and dusk are great times to spot wildlife and watch the light dance and the shadows shift on the canyon's walls. Be sure to set your alarm clock for an early start and make a beeline to either **Yavapai or Mather Point**. Both offer awesome views.

Let's Eat

It's always fun to **compare sunrise photos over breakfast.** Grab a quick meal at the **Maswik or Yavapai Lodge** cafeteria, or enjoy a fancier meal in the dining room at the historic **El Tovar Hotel**.

Mather Point

Feel the Burn

Now it's time to get some exercise to burn off those pancakes. You might start your adventure by visiting **Grand Canyon Visitor Center** near Mather Point. The National Park Service offers a free orientation movie, and you'll find friendly rangers to help plan your day.

You'll learn a lot by hanging out with the **rangers**. They give **talks** and lead group **hikes**. These programs are free, so go on as many as you'd like.

And, hey, while you're in the visitor center, sign up to become a **junior ranger!** Just pick up an activity brochure. Once you've completed your assignments, a ranger will swear you in as a junior ranger and give you a **Grand Canyon junior ranger certificate.** You can also buy an official patch to show all your friends back home.

There are more than a dozen spots along the South Rim where you can get out of the car and look out at the amazing view. A favorite for many is **Mather Point,** named after **Stephen Mather,** the first director of the National Park Service.

Stories in Stone

Want to learn more about the **rocks and how the canyon formed?** Check out the interesting exhibits and big views at the **Yavapai Geology Museum,** and then walk the **"Trail of Time,"** which begins just west of the museum on the Rim Trail. **With every step, you travel back in time almost 1 million years,** until you reach the very beginnings of Grand Canyon. (Phew! Be sure to stop, rest, and drink some water. Time travel is exhausting!)

Cool!

TRAIL OF TIME

ROCK CAPTURES TIME · TIME CARVES CANYON · CANYON REVEALS ROCK

Explore Ruins

Do you do chores back home? For **Ancestral Puebloan girls and boys,** chores may have included collecting firewood, weeding the crops, grinding corn between stones, or hauling water. Archaeologists learn these things by studying places like the **Tusayan Ruin,** an Ancestral Puebloan village.

Yikes!

Though nearly **5 million people visit the park each year,** only a fraction camp or stay in cabins below the rim. This number includes approximately 35,000 backpackers, 25,000 river runners, and 4,000 mule riders.

You'll finish your adventure at **Verkamp's Visitor Center,** where exhibits share the history of Grand Canyon Village. Here you can learn what it was like to **grow up living on the edge of Grand Canyon.**

The Daring Kolb Brothers

Brothers Emery and Ellsworth Kolb loved adventure. They created some of the first photographs ever taken in Grand Canyon. They built their **Kolb Studio** right on the very edge of the canyon.

Mary Jane Colter

Of the many architects responsible for building the **amazing historic structures** at Grand Canyon, none became more famous than **Mary Jane Colter.** Born in Minnesota in 1869, she went on to design the park's most admired buildings:

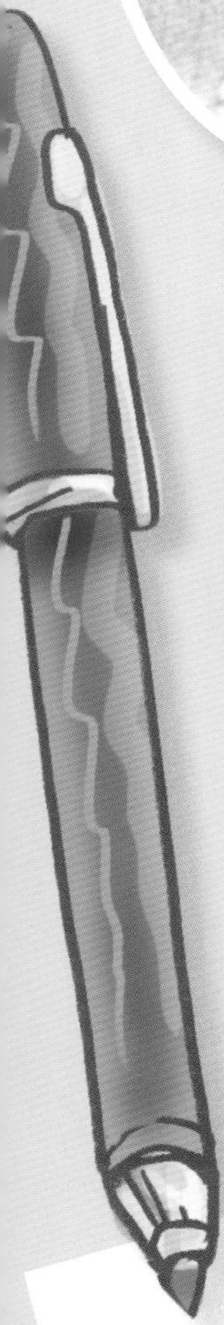

Desert View Watchtower

Lookout Studio

Hermits Rest

Phantom Ranch

Hopi House

Bright Angel Lodge

Dancers

On some summer afternoons you can often watch **American Indian dancers** performing near **Hopi House.** This is a tradition that dates back to the early 1900s.

More to Do

Guided bus tours, scenic helicopter flights, raft trips, mule rides along the rim or into the canyon, and guided hiking opportunities are offered by both non-profit and commercial operators. The park's website lists a number of these tours and activities (www.nps.gov/grca). Some require advance reservations.

Sunset at Yaki Point

Did you see that?

Plan on eating dinner early or after dark so that you can enjoy one of the **prettiest sunsets in the world.** Take a free park shuttle to either **Hopi or Yaki Point,** leaving enough time to pick a comfortable spot. These are two popular places to watch the sunset, but there is really not a bad seat in the house.

Also, be sure to look up at the **night sky** if you find yourself outdoors after dark. With few city lights, the **star viewing** in northern Arizona is truly stellar. If you're lucky, you might even see a **shooting star** or discover a **satellite** moving slowly across the sky.

What To Bring

water
(recommended 1 quart per person per hour)

hiking boots
(or other walking shoes with a stiff sole—sneakers are not great for long hikes)

layered clothing for wide-ranging temperatures

rain jacket or poncho

brimmed hat

sunscreen
(Remember to reapply!)

sunglasses

snacks

trail map

lightweight flashlight and extra batteries

small first-aid kit

camera

Not cool!

Finally, remember to **leave the park the way you found it.** By not littering or taking souvenir rocks, you'll be making sure that the next people who come along will have just as much fun as you had.

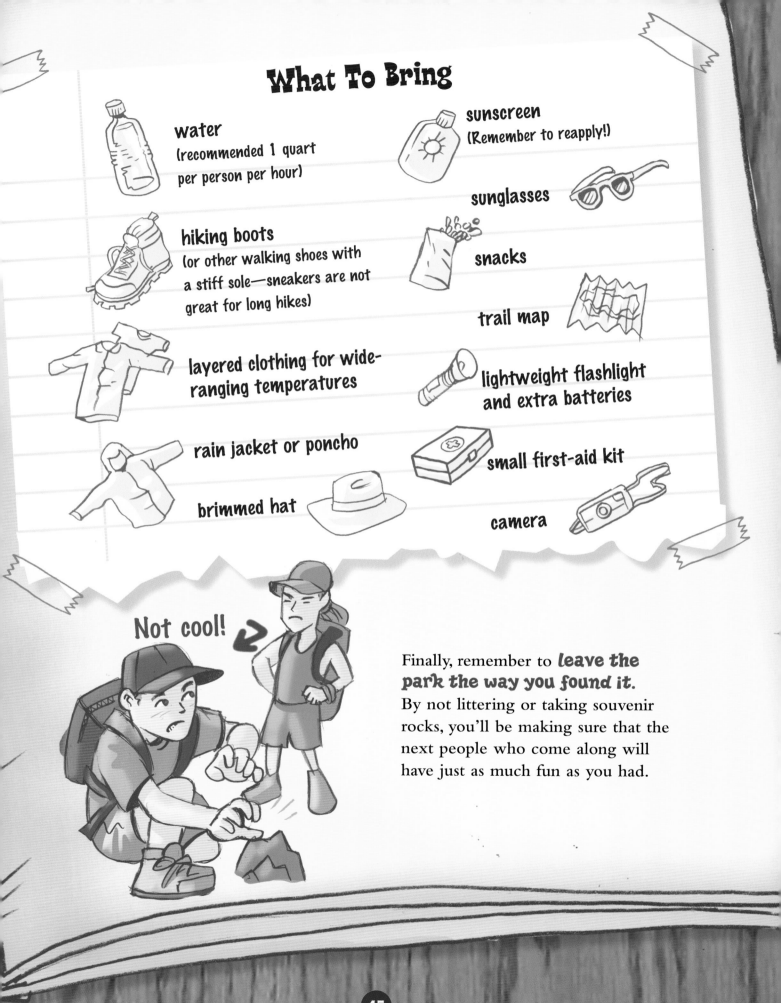

Photographers come from all over the world to capture the beauty of Grand Canyon. **Sunrise and sunset** are the best times to take photos because the light is perfect for catching rich colors, dramatic shadows, and great detail. Photographers call this the **"golden hour."**

If you're like most people, before you reach home you'll be planning your **return visit** to Grand Canyon National Park!

Credits

All illustrations by Robert Rath, www.robertrath.net.

Mike Buchheit: cover; scenic, page 12-13; Grand Canyon pink rattlesnake, page 20; Utah agave, page 28; pictograph and petroglyph, page 30.

Jacques Descloitres, MODIS Land Rapid Response Team, NASA/GSFC: Grand Canyon from space, page 5.

Grand Canyon National Park: stromatolite fossil, #GRCA 8323; fern, tracks, trilobite, tube worm, #fern_b, 2915, 11502, 8528, page 10; Vasey's Paradise, Park #D049, page 12; Ribbon Falls, #06950, page 12; Colorado River, #D0484, page 13; rafting, #D5697, page 13; humpback chub images, #Mathis 219, #Mathis 177, 290, 489, 2-057, page 14; scenic, #Mathis 2011_5067a, page 15; condor, #87_3467, page 21; cottonwood and prickly pear, #2849, page 28; Mormon tea, page 28; moss, #06942, page 28; artifacts, #GRCA 13539, GRCA 16424, 100-2445, 057-088-476-shell-bead_1647, 266-1-front-mineral_1456, page 29; split-twig figurine, #GRCA 30101b, page 29; Tusayan Pueblo, page 30; Billy Burro, #30736, page 31; John Wesley Powell, #17227, page 31; Kolb brothers, #17185B, page 31 and 37; El Tovar, #0542_0137, page 32 and 36; Phantom Ranch, #0322, page 33; Desert View Watchtowner, #0160, page 33; settlers, #17234, page 35; Harvey Girls, #18350, page 36; Kolb house, #4856, page 37; Mather Point, 2011_4096a, page 37; Mather Point, 2011_5067a, page 41; Junior Ranger badge, page 41; Tusayan Ruins, page 42; Trail of Time logo, page 42; Kolb brothers aerial tramway photo, 05435, page 42; Verkamp's, page 42; Desert View Watchtower, D0085; Lookout Studio, 0114; Hermit's Rest, 007; Bright Angel Lodge; Hopi House, 05539; Phantom Ranch, 2878, page 43; Mary Jane Colter, 16950, page 43; Yaki Point, 9517, page 44.

Sally King, National Park Service: pinyon jay, page 20; rock squirrel, page 20; Abert squirrel, page 20.

John Lambing: rainbow trout, page 22.

Library of Congress: Theodore Roosevelt, 3C28069U, page 38; Woodrow Wilson, 3A1763U, page 39.

Chuck and Betty Mulcahy, Imperial National Wildlife Refuge, AZ: pack rat midden, page 28.

Tom Mulvaney: postcard, page 35.

Northern Arizona University, Cline Library, Emery Kolb Collection: Edith Kolb, NAU.PH.568.8919, page 37.

Gaelyn Olmsted, http://geogypsy.blogspot.com: Kaibab squirrel, page 20.

Aacute Pest Control: bat guano, page 10.

Photos.com: mule, page 35.

Thinkstock: coyote howling, page 3; scenic, page 4-5; scenic, page 8-9; copper, silver, asbestos, page 10; sedimentary, igneous, and metamorphic rock, page, 9; Colorado River, page 13; scenic, page 14-15; Havasu Creek, page 15; elk, page 20; mule deer, page 20; gray fox, page 20; jackrabbit, page 20; collared lizard, page 20; coyote, page 20; mountain lion, page 21; copper, page 31; Havasu Falls, page 32; scenic, page 32-33; scenic, page 36-37; sunrise, page 40; sunset, page 46.

US Fish and Wildlife Service: bighorn sheep, page 20.

Richard Wagner / WildNaturePhotos: bark scorpion, page 22.

Index